Purpose

The material included in this publication has been prepared by the Professional Development Subcommittee of the Membership and Organization Committee of the International Reading Association for use as a staff development presentation. The subcommittee took its cue from the motion passed by the IRA Executive Board in its January 1988 meeting, which read in part as follows:

> Literature must be the foundation of the Language Arts Curriculum. Therefore, the Board of Directors endorses the replacement of worksheet activities requiring little reading and writing with the reading of and writing about fiction and nonfiction literature....

In response to this breakthrough by IRA, the Professional Development Subcommittee developed this document, which highlights activities designed to meet the requirement stated so strongly in that motion. The purpose of this document is to provide alternatives that not only require more reading and writing on the part of students, but also get them to think, focus on meaning, and consider the literary elements of a story. Activities included are classroom tested, may be tailored to fit each selection, may be accomplished in small or large groups, and may be used as an end in themselves or as a means to an end. They have been collected and adapted from various sources. In every case, credit has been given to the originator or source of the activity, although in some cases these people may themselves have adapted their ideas from similar activities used by others.

Included in this document are the following sections:

Rationale for Responses to Literature   Several theories of response to literature are covered, as is the crucial area of prior knowledge and the role it plays in response to literature. A brief survey of the research on response to literature is provided, including connections to several national and/or state publications on the topic.

Engagement Activities   A list of suitable activities with descriptions and examples is included. These activities bear the title "Engagement Activities" because their prime purpose is to absorb, immerse, and fully involve students in literature. In addition, the purpose of each activity is included, along with appropriate grade levels.

Management Issues   This section includes information on time allotments, scheduling, and classroom and schoolwide organization for a literature-based program. In addition, it deals with ways to provide for less able readers, as well as unit themes, resources, selection of material, and evaluation.

The contents of this publication are germane to districts/divisions that are just beginning to use literature in classrooms or that are in the process of implementing a comprehensive literature-based reading program. We are suggesting that Engagement Activities be applied when literature is being used to teach reading, such as from a core list of books. However, this does not preclude the reading of other literature selections by students for the sheer pleasure of enjoying a fine book. Helping students discover and delight in reading a good book prevails as a top priority for educators.

Presenter Information

The contents of this document are designed as a package to be presented to participants in small conferences or workshops. Overall, the Rationale for Responses to Literature provides the *why* for participants, the Engagement Activities section demonstrates the *what* for attendees, and the Management Issues part is devoted to *how* to implement the ideas presented.

Here are some suggestions for presenters:

- Be thoroughly familiar with each of the three parts of the document.
- If possible, have students try out some of the Engagement Activities prior to the presentation to provide the presenter with student work to display and discuss.
- Present the information to groups of about 50 or fewer to promote maximal interaction and discussion regarding the contents.
- Present the information to separate groups representing K-3 and 4-8, if this is feasible. Many of the activities are suitable for most levels, but a few fit better with lower or upper grades. Reducing the range of grade levels involved makes it easier to focus on the specific needs of those present.
- Types of presentations:

    Awareness sessions   These are usually an hour or so in length and, as a result, make it possible to cover in general terms only the ideas presented in the document. Therefore, participants will be hearing about the rationale, the activities, and the ways to manage the classroom rather than acquiring specific techniques.

    Workshop sessions   These are usually scheduled for periods ranging from two to four hours in length and therefore enable the participants to become involved in applying a number of the activities included. In other words, attendees reach the application level by working their way through activities. This presentation will have a much greater impact on students in the classroom, since teachers will be much more knowledgeable about the suggestions and activities and more willing to try them out.

Split workshop sessions   These sessions split the presentation into two or more parts, thereby making it possible to cover more of the material in the document as well as involve participants directly. Most of the same advantages of the workshop session apply in this procedure.

- Materials needed: Presenters will need to provide a copy of the materials for each participant. Also, the use of transparencies by the presenter greatly enhances the effectiveness of the presentation. Student work, if available, adds to the workshop immeasurably, as participants can view the "real thing."

Responses to Literature: Rationale

"A blessed thing happened to me as a child. I had a teacher who read to me" (Martin, 1987, p. 15). Bill Martin Jr's Miss Davis made a difference in his life because she was a lover of literature and shared great books with her students. Today, throughout the world, more and more teachers are spreading the word that literature should be shared, that children who read become better readers. Like Miss Davis, they believe in Ralph Waldo Emerson's adage, "'Tis the good reader that makes the good book."

During the past ten years, our understanding of the reading process has been enhanced by a plethora of research studies. Underlying this research have been primarily two theoretical models: schema theory and interactionist theory.

When readers comprehend a piece of text, they do so, in part, because of the prior knowledge they bring to the reading. Each person has schemata that have developed as a result of all their experiences. The individual's schemata are activated, with new information being integrated with old, thus forming a new or elaborated schemata (Tierney & Pearson, 1985). Schema theory suggests that readers comprehend when a bridge is built between prior knowledge and new information.

One type of schema children bring to the reading of literature is a sense of how a story functions, called story structure or story schema (Anderson & Pearson, 1984). When a child's understanding of story matches what he or she expects to occur, the bridge is built and, as a result, comprehension of the story is facilitated.

Interactionist theory contends that children learn language through interaction with all aspects of their environment (Genishi & Dyson, 1985). An interactionist perspective would suggest that, as teachers, we must work with the whole child, how he or she feels, how he or she thinks, what his or her genes have contributed, and what his or her social and physical environments provide. A child's interpretation of the text, then, depends upon his or her background. A practical implication here is that we cannot just search for "correct" answers. Rather, a reader's response to the work depends upon his or her interaction with the writer's words; it is this combination of "personal, social, and cultural contexts which have tremendous influence on the reader's interpretation" (Largent, 1986, p. 17).

How do these theories relate to our understanding of the reading process? Comprehension occurs when students can activate their prior knowledge and associate it with new knowledge gained from their reading. This linking of old and new knowledge is enhanced when all language processes (reading, writing, listening, speaking) are integrated and when students are reading interesting, aesthetically pleasing, and developmentally appropriate pieces of text.

Due to our new understandings, we now believe that this interactive, strategic use of language, especially as it relates to reading, can be best achieved when reading instruction occurs within the context of literature, rather than through the fragmentation and teaching of isolated skills. Therefore, skill instruction is incorporated into the reading of an entire piece of text, the whole poem, story, or book (Sawyer, 1987). Quality literature provides just such a context not only for pleasurable reading experiences but also for the development of reading skills (California State Department of Education, 1987). The International Reading Association, therefore, strongly urges its members to replace mindless worksheets that "drill and kill" with literature-based instruction that provides for the active engagement of readers.

In a literature-based reading program, teachers and children select appealing literature that reflects the real world. Teachers link students' prior experiences with stories, and instead of skill development activities, the reader's response to literature is encouraged. Opportunities are provided for the students to discuss and share, to write, and to listen to each other's interpretations and feelings about the story, novel, or poem.

Activities that precede and follow the reading must not be artificial exercises, but rather real communication opportunities that engage the reader's mind, interests, and feelings (Altwerger, Edelsky, & Flores, 1987). Thus, readers learn to respond to literature, to make judgments, to relate what they read to their own lives, and to "absorb the language of literature" (Cullinan, 1987, p. 4). When children are exposed to the rich images and interesting language that are found in quality literature, they become not only willing readers but also partners in the literary experiences of the characters they read about.

The activities included in this packet encourage students' responses to literature. They utilize prior experience, integrate all the language processes, and assist students in learning and using useful strategies for active comprehension of text; they truly *engage* the reader. Some Engagement Activities can be used prior to the reading of stories, others can be used as the reader progresses through the text, and others are most effective following reading. In essence, the suggested activities can be used to move students *into, through*, and *beyond* the text. Hopefully, they will encourage students to become lifelong readers whose sense of the aesthetic is enriched by contact with quality literature.

The section that follows describes, gives examples, and provides models for the various Engagement Activities. The final section in this publication deals with classroom management suggestions that enable classroom teachers to organize, manage, and direct their students toward maximal learning.

Responses to Literature: Engagement Activities

The purpose of Engagement Activities is to get students immersed, engrossed, absorbed, and totally involved in literature. We want students to experience the story from the inside out, not from the outside looking in. Students will not be dissecting the text, nor will they inspect it; rather, they will be focused on such literature elements as the main characters, the setting, the problem to be resolved, the major events, the problem solution, and what the story is really about. We hope the reader finds a spark of him/herself in each book and thus is able to connect the story to personal experiences.

Included in this publication are the following Engagement Activities:

Discussion	Knowledge Chart
Writing	Story Summary
Story Frame	Story Chart
Plot Relationships Chart	Character Map
Story Map	Compare/Contrast Chart (Venn Diagram)
Prediction Chart	Story Pyramid

The teacher makes the decision regarding which activities are best suited to a particular selection, thus tailoring the activities to the text. Discussion is always in order, as promoted by this comment by Mortimer Adler: "Books not discussed lose their value." Additional writing responses may be included even though many of the Engagement Activities include much writing. Caution against *overusing* Engagement Activities is advised, as too many activities can turn off students and make them indifferent to literature.

For maximum learning to occur, the teacher must teach students how to do the activities assigned. Learning works well when teachers select an easy book or story, read it aloud to students (or have upper grade students read it on their own), and "walk students through" the activity, modeling the manner in which the activity is developed, completed, and used. For example, *Herbie's Troubles* by Carol Chapman is an excellent primary book to use when teaching the Story Pyramid; *Piggybook* by Anthony Browne works well for the Story Map. Once students have acquired the skills needed, they proceed with the activity as outlined by the teacher. Activities may be completed by individual students, by cooperative learning groups, or by an entire class. The teacher and the grade level involved determine the best way to proceed.

Engagement Activities may be used as an end in themselves or, better yet, as a means to an end. Just completing the assigned activities will enable students to achieve full comprehension of the story. However, when the responses generated in the various activities are used as a springboard for discussion or writing, comprehension truly flourishes. Students must understand that they should complete the assigned reading *prior* to tackling the assigned activity rather than interrupting the flow of the story to record their data. Preserve the integrity of the text, then work on the activities. Enjoyment of literature remains paramount!

When students read or hear literature, they should do something of value as follow-up, particularly when literature is being used to teach reading. Engagement Activities will serve not only to integrate the language arts but also to promote cultural literacy.

Discussion—An Indispensable Activity

Discussion is an integral part of a quality reading program, especially when it is literature based. When students are engaged in a lively discussion of a literature selection, their comprehension of that selection is greatly enhanced, not only through thoughtful questions posed by the teacher but also through interaction with other students in the discussion process. Student-led discussions are also most productive, as outlined by Palincsar and Brown (1985) in their reciprocal reading process. Full comprehension may make it possible for students to relate the work being discussed to their own lives, their specific situations, and their own set of problems or concerns, and this connection may bring on personal growth and maturity.

Discussion is not recitation, nor is it interrogation! It takes considerable skill and design to be most productive. Listed below are suggestions for conducting successful teacher-led discussions:

● The teacher's role becomes one of facilitator or orchestrator, keeping the discussion moving, on task, and promoting interaction.

● The teacher should use a list of prepared questions in leading a discussion but be ready to pose questions that may be triggered by a student response or comment.

● The teacher should include all levels of thinking in facilitating the discussion. Any taxonomy—Bloom, Taba, Guilford, Barrett—can be of considerable value if implemented correctly.

- Discussion groups may vary in size from six to eight students to an entire class; however, groups comprising more than twelve to fifteen students will be less effective.
- The teacher must provide a pause, or "wait time," of five or more seconds before expecting a response in order to give students time to do their best creative and active thinking before making an overt response. Adhere to this strategy when students are interacting with one another, also. Explain this strategy to students beforehand.
- If answers differ when literal, knowledge, or recall level questions are asked, consult the text to locate appropriate data.
- The teacher should involve all students in the discussion by calling on them if necessary or encouraging them to offer a response.
- After a student responds to a question, the teacher should behave in a manner designed to advance the discussion rather than terminate it. Such responses on the part of the teacher as "Okay," "Um hm," "Got it," or "Thanks" will keep answers coming. On the other hand, negative response behaviors such as criticism or excessive praise stifle a discussion. In promoting discussion, prompting, delving, and summarizing can aid a student in generating a thoughtful response.
- Audiotaping a discussion and subsequent analysis by the teacher/students will provide a valuable record of successful as well as unsuccessful discussions.

Writing—Its Connection to Reading

Traditionally, reading has been viewed as a passive decoding process and writing as an active encoding process. These views have led to separate curricula and even to separate teaching strategies for the various reading and writing skills.

However, both the reading and writing processes are acts of composing, and they are interrelated, with the goal of each being the construction of meaning. The writer, through the act of writing and with a sense of purpose and audience, creates a message to be read. But, as Joseph Conrad stated, "One writes only half the book; the other half is with the reader." The reader, then, composes meaning from the writer's words, attending to the author's purpose while integrating the newly read material with his or her own background knowledge.

Common sense might tell us that it is important to have students write while they read and read while they write; research findings also support the notion that children who are better writers also tend to be better readers. Similarly, those who are better readers tend to be better writers. Intelligence is also a causal factor in these two processes.

Children's and adolescent literature can provide models of effective writing, can serve as springboards for writing activities, can expand background knowledge, and can, of course, stimulate thinking. During many of these writing experiences, the *response* to the reading and writing is the goal, not perfection in grammar and punctuation.

To engage students' minds and interests through a written response to literature, teachers might try the following:

- Become a model reader/writer yourself. Let your students see you write after you read; let them see you struggle through the planning, writing, and revising stages. Share with them what you have written. Ask their advice about editorial changes they would make in your work.
- Facilitate peer response groups whereby partners or small groups share, edit, and revise their writings together. The purpose here is not to correct each other's work, but rather to clarify ideas and work toward cogent thinking on the part of all group members.
- Implement journal writing such as dialogue journals between students in the same or different grade levels. The students can respond to common reading assignments or books they are both enjoying. They can discuss their own lives as well as those of the characters they are studying. Children as young as first grade can take part in invented spelling dialogue journals; parents, older students, or aides can assist in translation, if necessary. One junior high teacher keeps a dialogue journal on her desk, and each student, throughout the day, makes a literary contribution.
- Provide for writing conference time each week whereby each student has a chance to pow-wow with the teacher about his or her writing success and concerns.
- When you display student writing, don't limit the displays to the perfect, revised papers. Also display works in progress, so students can see that writing is a *process*, not just something the "smart kids" crank out without effort.
- Turn your classroom into a publishing empire. Whether your students write and produce simple construction paper books, Big Books, or ornate clothbound books, celebrate reading and writing by turning children's writing into books that can be read and enjoyed by others.
- Employ the Five-Minute Write technique. Prior to introducing a story or content lesson, students write in paragraph form everything they know about the topic to be read. After five minutes, ask them to jot down any questions that came to mind during the writing. Have them mark with a + any questions they think could be answered by their reading. Students then share their written work with each other. During the reading, students record answers to any questions that were previously generated. Discussion of story, paragraphs, and questions/answers can follow. Unanswered questions can be ideal research topics.

Story Frame
by G.L. Fowler

Purpose To focus the reader on basic story content, including the setting and the main characters.

Grade Levels Regular students in primary grades; less able readers in middle and upper grades.

Description The Story Frame requires that a student focus on the main characters, the setting, the major events, and the conclusion in a story. Enough information is given in the frame to enable students to put together the basic information required. In primary grades, the teacher will want to work with students as a class or in smaller groups and develop the Story Frame with student input. In middle and upper grades, less prepared readers can complete the activity on their own, filling in the essential information. *The Story Frame may be simplified or made more complex by reducing or increasing the number of main events in the story that are to be included.* It is an excellent device to use with students who need to work with basic information in a story in order to comprehend the idea of story grammar and to apply this concept to an appropriate literature selection.

Sample Story Frame for *Cinderella,* by Charles Perrault

The story takes place *in a make believe kingdom where Cinderella lives with her stepmother and sisters in a nice house* .

Cinderella, a stepsister, is a character in the story who *has to do all the chores around the house like a servant* .

The fairy godmother is another character in the story who *does magic and helps Cinderella go the to ball* .

A problem occurs when *Cinderella is hurrying home at midnight and drops one of her glass slippers at the ball* .

After that, *the handsome prince searches in the kingdom for a young lady who can put on the glass slipper and have it fit,* and *the shoe doesn't fit any of the young ladies who try it on* .

The problem is solved when *Cinderella tries on the glass slipper, and it fits perfectly* .

The story ends with *the handsome prince and Cinderella getting married right away, and they live happily ever after* .

Story Frame

The story takes place _____

_____ .

_____ is a character in the story

who _____ .

_____ is another character in the

story who _____ .

A problem occurs when _____

_____ .

After that, _____

_____

and _____ .

The problem is solved when _____

_____ .

The story ends with _____

_____ .

The teacher may wish to make the Story Frame simpler by providing space for only one character and fewer major events in the story. On the other hand, the teacher may desire to make the outline more complicated by adding more spaces for additional characters and events. Also, the teacher may want to vary the space provided for the various entries. He or she no doubt will want to tailor the Story Frame to fit a specific title, thereby providing a more prescriptive outline, once he or she becomes more familiar with the activity.

Plot Relationships Chart
by Barbara Schmidt and Marilyn Buckley

Purpose   To focus readers on problem-solution elements of the selection; to develop a sense of story; to perceive the relationships between and among selection elements; and to provide a basis for oral and written extension of these elements.

Grade Levels   Primary grades; less prepared readers in middle and upper grades.

Description   The Plot Relationships Chart requires that students identify the major elements of a selection they have heard or read. Use of the chart should first be modeled by the teacher, who demonstrates the relationship of the elements as students dictate. An emphasis should be placed on encouraging students to perceive the relationships between characters, goal, problem, and solution. A discussion on alternative solutions is a logical extension. The four guide words (Somebody, Wanted, But, and So) provide the structure enabling students to work through the task. To reinforce the structure, the teacher can have the class develop its own chart. Several applications should be modeled before students use the structure with partners or in collaborative groups. The Plot Relationships Chart provides a useful skeleton for oral and written elaboration. Students might be encouraged to use this format to share personal reading, to generate original story ideas, to describe the plots of favorite TV shows or movies, or to relate current events. The Plot Relationships Chart is a step up in difficulty from the Story Frame and is designed to give the reader an opportunity to use his or her own language and ideas.

Sample Plot Relationships Chart for *Stone Fox*, by John Reynolds Gardiner

Somebody	Wanted	But	So
Little Willie	to win the dogsled race and earn the first prize of $500 so he could pay the back taxes on Grandpa's farm.	Stone Fox, a Shoshone Indian, enters the race with his dog team of Samoyeds so he can win the $500 prize and buy back lands his tribe has lost.	Little Willie and Stone Fox race, and close to the finish line when they are neck-and-neck, Willie's dog, Searchlight, drops dead from exhaustion. Stone Fox lets Willie carry Searchlight across the finish line and win the $500 prize.

Plot Relationships Chart

Somebody	Wanted	But	So

Story Map
by Isabel Beck

Purpose   To provide literary essentials such as the main characters, the setting, the problem, the major events, the problem solution, and the theme for a story.

Grade Levels   Regular and less prepared students in grades K-8.

Description   A Story Map helps students glean essential data from a story. In this activity, students complete the Story Map as a whole class or reading group in primary grades, writing the required information in the space provided. Middle and upper grade students can fill in the outline on their own. Less prepared students may need assistance with ideas and procedures. Some guidance in deciding the main events in the story may be necessary, or students may include too many facts. Students need to learn to combine like events, give them a broader title, then proceed. In completing the Story Map, students should first listen to the entire story, if it is being read aloud. If they are reading the story or a book in parts or segments, they should complete the assigned portion prior to filling in the Story Map. Otherwise, they will lose the thread of the story or interrupt its flow by stopping to insert data in the Story Map. The completed Story Map provides much material for discussion or writing, whichever is most appropriate for the literary selection being used.

Sample Story Map for *Molly's Pilgrim*, by Barbara Cohen

Setting/main characters	Home and school. Molly, Mama, Miss Stickley, Elizabeth.
Statement of the problem	The other children laugh at and make fun of Molly.

Event 1	The children tease Molly.
Event 2	The class has to make Pilgrim clothespin dolls.
Event 3	Mama makes Molly's doll look like herself.
Event 4	The children laugh at Molly's doll because it doesn't look like a Pilgrim.
Event 5	The teacher tells about modern Pilgrims and the Jewish holiday that inspired Thanksgiving.

Statement of the solution	The children understand about Molly and decide to be friends with her.
Story theme (What is this story *really* about?)	People are different, but when you get to know them, you often like them.

Story Map

The setting/main characters

Statement of the problem

Event 1

Event 2

Event 3

Event 4

Event 5

Event 6

Event 7

Statement of the solution

Story theme (What is this story *really* about?)

Values brought out in the story

Prediction Chart
by Dorsey Hammond

Purpose To provide students with more formal opportunities to predict what will happen in a story and compare their prediction with what actually happened.

Grade Levels Very appropriate for students K-8. In primary grades and with less able readers, teacher direction and assistance will be needed in developing a group chart. In grades 4-8, students can complete Prediction Charts alone or in cooperative groups.

Description All good readers predict what will happen next as they move through a story. When Prediction Charts are used, three things occur for students: prior knowledge is activated, a purpose for reading is established, and students are motivated to support or refute their prediction. Initially, the teacher discusses the cover of a book, the title, and other pertinent data of a general nature. Students then predict in writing what they think will happen in the first chapter or segment assignment. After they complete the assigned reading, they summarize what actually happened. As students move through the story, predictions tend to become more accurate as students gain experience, pick up foreshadowing clues, and activate their prior knowledge about what has happened so far. While students strive to match predictions with outcomes, a basic purpose of this activity is to heighten motivation and interest in reading quality material on the part of readers. Enthusiastic readers become willing readers who experience literature through this close engagement with it.

Sample Prediction Chart for *The Trouble with Tuck*, by Theodore Taylor

	What I predict will happen	What actually happened
Part 1 pp. 1-18	Answers will vary.	Helen and her family decide Tuck's vision is bad. Then, in a flashback, Helen and Tuck are described, and Tuck gets his name.
Part 2 pp. 19-36	Answers will vary.	Tuck saves Helen from an attacker in the park and also saves her from drowning. The family decides that Tuck must be taken to the vet to see just what his problem is.
Part 3 pp. 37-63	Answers will vary.	The vet confims Tuck's blindness and offers no hope. Tuck continues to have problems. Helen thinks of a companion dog, but she is told that none is available for dogs, only people.
Part 4 pp. 64-82	Answers will vary.	Tuck is tied up with a rope, then a chain after fences don't keep him safe. Helen thinks her parents are going to put him to sleep and runs away with Tuck, but finds out later that she was mistaken.
Part 5 pp. 83-110	Answers will vary.	Daisy, a retired seeing-eye dog, comes to help Helen with Tuck. Through Helen's love and perseverance, the two dogs learn to work together. This time Helen saves Tuck's life; she is happier than ever.

Prediction Chart

	What I predict will happen	What actually happened
Chapter 1		
Chapter 2		
Chapter 3		
Chapter 4		
Chapter 5		
Chapter 6		

Knowledge Chart
by Jim and Joan Macon

Purpose   To enable the reader to activate prior knowledge concerning a specific topic, then listen to or read about that topic, and finally list new knowledge gained.

Grade Levels   Regular students in primary, middle, and upper grades; less prepared readers in the middle and upper grades.

Description   The Knowledge Chart is a very versatile Engagement Activity that can be used in a variety of settings. A good strategy is to have students pool their information about a certain topic, clustering it on the chalkboard, a transparency, or on paper, thereby making it available to all students. However, encouraging individual students to access their own prior knowledge is also an effective practice. You may wish to vary the procedure. After a plan is adopted, students read or listen to a selection on the same topic, with students listing new knowledge gained individually or in a group, or with the teacher doing so. The Knowledge Chart works best if students have some knowledge about the topic but don't know a great deal. If no prior knowledge exists, the teacher must build a knowledge bridge by discussing similar topics or information. This activity is also very effective with nonfiction materials. After the prior knowledge and new knowledge have been recorded and discussed, the teacher may move into the scheduled lesson, since a knowledge bridge now exists.

Sample Knowledge Chart for *Strega Nona,*
by Tomie dePaola

Prior knowledge about _____ witches _____	New knowledge about _____ witches _____
1. wear pointy black hats	1. do good things (cure headaches, etc.)
2. ride a broom	2. sing to a pot
3. stir a witch's pot	3. blow kisses
4. cast magic spells	4. give out fair punishment
5. have a black cat	5. have friends
6. wear pointy shoes	
7. have an ugly face	

Knowledge Chart

Prior knowledge about _____	New knowledge about _____
1.	1.
2.	2.
3.	3.
4.	4.
5.	5.
6.	6.
7.	7.
etc.	etc.

Story Summary
by Marian Davies Toth

Purpose To enable students to summarize chapters or segments assigned in order to enhance comprehension of story content.

Grade Levels Especially for students in grades 4-8, but also very useful with primary or less prepared students with teacher guidance. Story Summaries work especially well when students are organized into cooperative learning groups.

Description In the Story Summary students read each chapter or segment of an assigned story, then summarize that part. Students can do this on their own in upper grades, and with teacher help in primary grades or with less able readers. It is especially effective when the class is set up in cooperative learning groups. In this arrangement each student in the group is asked to write a two- to four-sentence summary of the chapter or segment. Results are then discussed and compared. The teacher can ask each group to come up with one summary. Once groups have accomplished this, the next step is to challenge students to reduce their summary further. This task is going to require a great deal of thinking, combining, casting out, and polishing to achieve the objective. Then the teacher can ask each group to share its final result, and ask the class to comment on strengths and weaknesses of each summary. Much learning can result from such discussions. An advanced assignment might require groups to develop summaries in the same manner, but this time for the entire book. Summaries can provide a number of opportunities for writing and discussion activities.

Sample Story Summary for *Treasure Island,* by Robert Louis Stevenson

Part 1	The main characters—Jim, Black Dog, Pew, Billy Bones, Dr. Livesey, and Squire Trelawney—are introduced. After Jim thwarts Black Dog and Pew, he discovers what could be a treasure map in Bones's sea chest. The Doctor and the Squire are excited about the map and, with Jim, make plans to outfit a ship and seek the buried treasure. The Squire leaves for the seaport of Bristol to begin preparations.
Part 2	The Squire, with Long John Silver's assistance, signs on the crew, much to the displeasure of Capt. Smollett, who "smells a rat." Jim overhears Silver and most of the crew plotting a mutiny when the time is ripe in order to get the gold for themselves. Immediately, he reports this information to Capt. Smollett, who devises a plan to "lay low" because the mutineers outnumber those loyal to the Captain. He will bide his time. Jim becomes an informer.
Part 3	With the Captain's permission, Silver and some of the crew go ashore to explore Treasure Island, and during this look-around "do in" several loyal crew members. Jim sneaks ashore and sees Silver doing his foul deeds. Then he discovers Ben Gunn, who was marooned by Capt. Flint's crew when the treasure was buried. They agree to help one another since they both want to leave the island with a share of the treasure.
Part 4	Capt. Smollett decides the stockade on the island is a better place to confront Silver and his men, so they abandon the *Hispaniola*, fortify themselves at the stockade, and prepare for the battle. In the battle Silver's men are beaten back, but only after much bloodshed on both sides. The odds are now four men for the Captain and nine with Silver—better than they were before, but still long.
Part 5	After the defeat of Silver, Jim takes off on another wild adventure—this time to beach the *Hispaniola* so Silver can't use it to leave the island. During this exciting experience, he is aided by mutineer Israel Hands, who tries to kill Jim but is himself shot and killed by Jim at the top of a mast. Jim then returns to the stockade only to be captured by Silver, who has taken over the fort.
Part 6	The mutineers want to get rid of Silver and give him the "black spot," but he calms them down by producing the treasure map. They proceed to search for the treasure and locate the site, but to no avail—the treasure is gone! Just as Silver is about to be attacked by the mutineers, shots from the Doctor, the Squire, and Gunn ring out, killing the attackers. Gunn, who had dug up and stowed the treasure in his cave, helps the crew load it aboard the *Hispaniola*. Capt. Smollett and the crew sail back to England and divide up the treasure, while Silver disappears.

Story Summary

Chapter 1	
Chapter 2	
Chapter 3	
Chapter 4	
Chapter 5	
Chapter 6	

Story Chart
by Sally Haskell

Purpose To make readers focus on the essentials in the story, thereby increasing their comprehension and analysis of the story.

Grade Levels Useful with primary and less prepared students with teacher help and guidance. In grades 4-8, students may complete the chart on their own or in cooperative learning groups.

Description The teacher uses the basic design in the Story Chart and gives each square a title. Titles are selected by the teacher because of their importance in the story, and because the teacher wants students to focus on these areas and generate full comprehension of each one. Titles will vary with each story, although some of them will remain the same, e.g., main characters, setting, the problem, resolution of the problem, and theme. Students read a chapter or segment of a story, then begin filling in the chart. By the end of the story they should have completed the chart and made the necessary conclusions. In class or small group discussions, students share their chart or part of it, depending on the teacher's purpose or the time available. In another strategy the teacher puts the basic design, including titles for a specific book, on large pieces of butcher paper and has students add their information (no duplications). When this task is completed, the possibilities for discussion and writing are virtually limitless. This is one of the most comprehensive and challenging Engagement Activities available to students, and is invaluable in developing a high level of story comprehension.

Sample Story Chart for *The Tale of Peter Rabbit,* by Beatrix Potter

Peter	Mr. McGregor	Mrs. Rabbit	Flopsy, Mopsy, Cottontail
• very naughty • disobedient • irresponsible • ate forbidden vegetables – got sick • cautious when in trouble • good thinker on his feet	• did not like rabbits in garden • had eaten rabbit pie recently • had a green thumb • handy (tool shed)	• dedicated, concerned mother • raised four rabbits by herself • busy	• good little bunnies • dependable
		Mr. Rabbit • had an "accident" in Mr. McGregor's garden	**Old mouse, cat** • found a pea in garden • lazy • no help to Peter
Setting • sandbank, Mr. McGregor's garden	**Problem** • How was Peter to get out of the garden safely?	**Problem solution** • slipped under the gate when Mr. McGregor wasn't looking	**What is this story really about?** • doing what your mother tells you to do
Values brought out in the story • obedience • responsibility	**Expressive language** • "lippity, lippity" • "implored him to exert himself" • "scritch, scratch"	**Good read-aloud parts** • "Stop thief!" • when Peter has to drink camomile tea and others get bread, milk, berries	

Story Chart

Character Map
by Marian Davies Toth

Purpose   To focus on main characters in a story, identifying their qualities or traits based on their actions in the story.

Grade levels   Best for grades 4-8, where students can work independently or in cooperative learning groups. May be used in primary grades or with the less prepared readers with teacher direction and assistance.

Description   Character Maps are extremely useful in assisting students to develop a more thorough understanding of characters in a story and the actions they take that lead to the identification of character traits. In the map students either write the name of the main characters in the square or paste in a picture from a magazine that they feel typifies the character in their mind. In the ovals students record qualities such as courage, perseverance, and loyalty, and in the circles they list the actions in the story that support those characteristics. Students complete the map as they go through the story but should read the chapter or segment assigned before they stop to fill in the map. It is important to maintain the flow, continuity, and integrity of the text, rather than stop periodically to fill in the map. *Students may add ovals and/or circles to the map as they discover more data that fit.* One of the best uses of a Character Map occurs when a story has two central characters, and students complete Character Maps on each of them. These data then provide for compare/contrast or other writing activities. Completed Character Maps also summarize a story.

Sample Character Map for *The Sign of the Beaver,* by Elizabeth George Speare

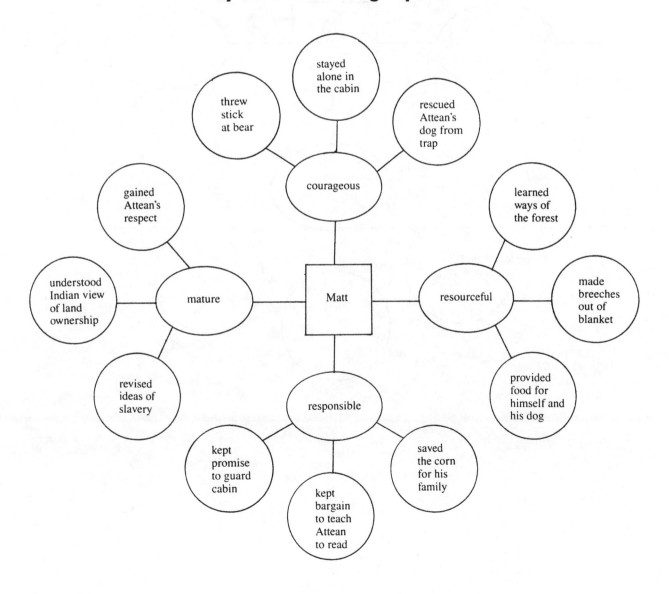

Character Map

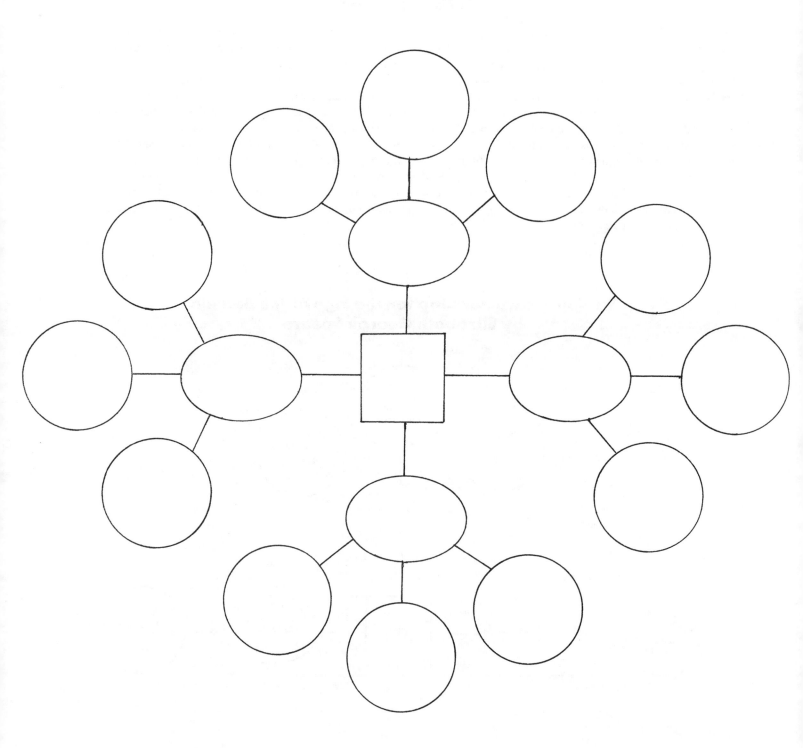

Compare/Contrast Chart
(Venn Diagram)

Purpose   To enable students to increase their comprehension of a story by analyzing likenesses and differences in characters, events, and outcomes, or to compare/contrast several similar stories.

Grade levels   Suitable for all levels, K-8. In primary grades, the teacher helps students develop a Venn Diagram by eliciting ideas from them and placing their information on a chart. The teacher would also function as facilitator in working with less prepared students. In grades 4-8, students could work individually or in cooperative learning groups.

Description   In a Compare/Contrast Chart students know that they compare things for likenesses and contrast things for differences. In completing the Venn Diagram, primary and less prepared students will do the thinking and the teacher will write down their responses. In grades 4-8, the class can work as individuals or in cooperative learning groups, and complete the diagram accordingly. Charts can then be shared through discussion, placed on large pieces of butcher paper, or put on transparencies for additional comparisons. In addition, the teacher may draw a large Venn Diagram on the chalkboard or butcher paper and ask students to fill in their information (no duplications). Once these data are in place, the teacher has a quantity of information for further discussions or writing assignments.

Sample Compare/Contrast Chart for
The Indian in the Cupboard, by Lynn Reid Banks,
and *The Castle in the Attic*, by Elizabeth Winthrop

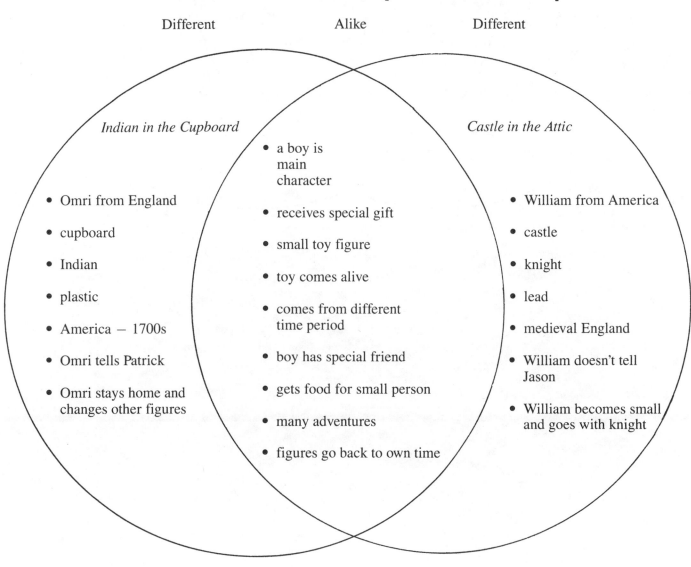

Different   Alike   Different

Indian in the Cupboard   *Castle in the Attic*

- Omri from England
- cupboard
- Indian
- plastic
- America — 1700s
- Omri tells Patrick
- Omri stays home and changes other figures

- a boy is main character
- receives special gift
- small toy figure
- toy comes alive
- comes from different time period
- boy has special friend
- gets food for small person
- many adventures
- figures go back to own time

- William from America
- castle
- knight
- lead
- medieval England
- William doesn't tell Jason
- William becomes small and goes with knight

Compare/Contrast Chart

Different   Alike   Different

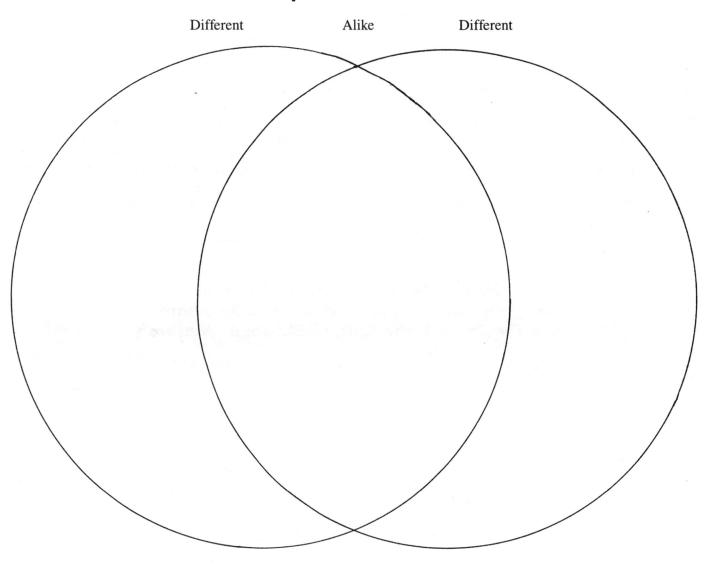

Story Pyramid
by Brenda Waldo

Purpose   To provide a vehicle for students to state who the main characters are, what the setting is, what the problem is, the main events in the story, and the resolution of the problem.

Grade Levels   More suited to grades 4-8, since students will need to know how to select the highlights of a story, using the literary essentials mentioned above but employing a limited number of words. It is also usable in primary grades, but the teacher must work directly with students for best results and develop a group Story Pyramid.

Description   In the Story Pyramid students are asked to complete a pyramid-shaped outline, which will include the following information:

Line 1.   Name of the main character
Line 2.   Two words describing the main character
Line 3.   Three words describing the setting
Line 4.   Four words stating the problem
Line 5.   Five words describing one main event
Line 6.   Six words describing a second main event
Line 7.   Seven words describing a third main event
Line 8.   Eight words stating the solution to the problem

At first glance this activity may appear to be too rigid. On further scrutiny, it is apparent that student answers may vary, and the central challenge of the activity is the selection of quality vocabulary to complete the design. Knowledge of story content plus the demand for just the right words stretches thinking and requires that students make cogent responses using an economy of words.

Sample Story Pyramid for *Julie of the Wolves*, by Jean Craighead George

1. Julie

2. brave   perplexed

3. Alaskan   towns/   wilderness

4. Retain/   abandon   "old   ways"

5. Julie   lives   with   wolf   pack

6. Julie   runs   away   from   "dumb"   husband

7. Julie   lives   with   father   in   Alaskan   village

8. Julie   decides   to   abandon   "old   ways"   for   civilization

Story Pyramid

1. _____

2. _____ _____

3. _____ _____ _____

4. _____ _____ _____ _____

5. _____ _____ _____ _____ _____

6. _____ _____ _____ _____ _____ _____

7. _____ _____ _____ _____ _____ _____ _____

8. _____ _____ _____ _____ _____ _____ _____ _____

1. Name of main character
2. Two words describing main character
3. Three words describing setting
4. Four words stating problem
5. Five words describing one event
6. Six words describing second event
7. Seven words describing third event
8. Eight words stating solution

_____
Student

_____
Name of Book

_____
Author

Responses to Literature:
Management Issues and Other Practical Concerns

In order to implement the use of literature in the classroom, educators will need to address a number of management issues, such as school and classroom organization, time allocation and scheduling, the development of themes and units, strategies, and evaluation procedures. It will be necessary to consider questions appropriate not only to the needs of individuals but also to the needs, requirements, and resources characteristic of many diverse geographical regions. Some of the issues that may arise and that demand resolution are included in the following questions:

1. Where do you find time for students to read and respond to literature through Engagement Activities?

In many cases, time constraints will not be an issue, but some teachers may find that suggestions related to the scheduling of reading time and Engagement Activities are needed. In areas where the use of basal programs is mandated, teachers may feel insecure about reducing the amount of time devoted to basal and workbook activities. They need to be reassured that it is not necessary to throw out the basal, only to reduce the amount of time spent on it. There is a range of alternatives, from the inclusion of children's literature in a basal-dominated program to the use of tradebooks in thematic units. Here are some sample options for consideration:

- Reduce the number of worksheets used during each period. In *Becoming a Nation of Readers* (Anderson et al., 1985) it is stated that up to 70 percent of the typical reading period may be spent on worksheets and workbooks. Clearly, this is an area where much time could be reallocated to the pursuit of literature.
- Allocate the morning to basal activities and the afternoon to literature activities (possibly integrated with other content/ subject areas).
- Allocate basal and literature/Engagement Activities to alternate days.
- Use basal themes as a springboard for literature/Engagement Activities conducted in basal time slots.
- Teach basal objectives in basal time slots, using literature/Engagement Activities rather than the basal reader and workbook.

2. How do you organize the program schoolwide?

This process is an important one and can be accomplished in a number of ways. Regarding the selection of literature materials, sometimes titles are determined by state/provincial mandate, with lists of books and activities appropriate for each grade level being developed by a "committee of experts." While this action relieves the individual teacher of the task of text selection, it fails to make use of teacher expertise. Fortunately, this is not often the case. Another means of text selection involves districts/divisions developing their own lists from a set of suggested books, using agreed upon selection criteria. As a rule, teachers are part of the selection process and can help ensure good choices. Also, in some areas teachers are free to make use of quality literature as determined by themselves. This opportunity places considerable responsibility on the classroom teacher but provides much more freedom of choice for students in the long run.

Regardless of the procedure employed to determine which books to use in a literature program, it is imperative that the best materials available be selected and used appropriately with students. One means of identifying literature selections for the classroom is to develop three lists. One list, the *core list*, comprises the books used to teach reading; a supplementary list, sometimes called the *extended list*, includes books designed to support the core list. A third list, the *recreational list*, may be identified as free time reading for students, with materials being utilized from school and public libraries.

It is obvious that there are several ways to identify literature for classroom use, with the policies of states, provinces, districts, and/or divisions providing direction. The central aim of any procedure must be to secure real books so students can become real readers.

3. How can you use themes to organize a literature centered program?

Organizing literature study through the development of thematic units is a powerful management strategy. The sources of themes are many and varied. They may be related to topics suggested by basal programs, student and/or teacher interests, current events, the calendar, science, social science, or mandated curricula. They provide wonderful opportunities for the integration of content area subjects as well as art, music, and physical education, and they can lead to a variety of grouping options. Students may work as individuals, as partners, in small cooperative learning groups, or in large groups.

Thematic units require careful planning, from the overview to the specific Engagement Activities to be accomplished. When teachers develop units collaboratively, they can tailor the unit to their own students, achieve genuine ownership, and increase their professional skills immeasureably. Commercially prepared units should be reviewed for ideas and possibilities, but care must be exercised to ensure that borrowed strategies are of high quality and meet curricular objectives. One approach to the development of a thematic unit includes the following steps:

- Determine and state the major concepts and ideas to be developed in the unit. These concepts and ideas should be related to curricular objectives. Engagement Activities make better sense when they are in concert with clearly defined goals. The amount of time allotted to the unit will depend on the concepts to be developed and should be established during the initial planning stage. Units lasting two to four weeks should provide ample time for comprehensive development and curriculum integration. Evaluation strategies should also be considered at this time; these should include both formative and summative procedures.

- Gather resources to be used in exploring and developing the concepts. A Resource Catalog is an invaluable tool to use when resources are being gathered. The catalog could be set up on a single sheet of paper. After listing the theme, dates, and objectives of the unit, available resources can be listed in the following categories: books/magazines, posters/charts, audiovisual material, resource people, and field trips. The length of time allotted to the unit will naturally affect the amount of resources required.
- Construct lessons and activities. Many sample Engagement Activities are included in the second section of this publication. When lessons and activities are being planned, management issues should also be considered. Teachers should provide a balance among large group, small group, partner, and individual activities, with scheduling issues given sufficient consideration. Students should be provided with a schedule that allows for the following (Rhodes, 1983):

planning time	silent reading time	writing workshops
work periods	journal/log writing	discussion/sharing time
story time	evaluation time	review time

Students should be informed about the products they will be expected to achieve as well as evaluation criteria. It is at this time that consideration should be given to the physical organization of the classroom itself. There is likely to be a need for work areas/centers that will accommodate the lessons and activities planned.

- Work through the unit with your students.
- Evaluate the effectiveness of the unit. There are at least three crucial questions that should be asked when evaluating the effectiveness of a thematic unit:

Did the students grow relative to the concepts and ideas that the unit was designed to develop?
Was the unit itself successful in facilitating student growth?
Was instruction effective in facilitating student progress?

Possibly the most important feedback to receive from students relates to their enjoyment of the unit. Are they eager to engage themselves in another quality unit, or have they been burned out by too many activities (overkill)?

4. How can groups be structured to ensure that effective learning takes place?

Small groups can be a powerful device to facilitate response to literature through Engagement Activities and cooperative learning strategies if the management plan permits all students at all ability levels to respond actively and to experience success. The use of a simple "jigsaw strategy" is one example of an effective means of providing students with a cooperative learning experience. Here is an outline of the procedure:

- Divide students into home groups of four to five members.
- Give a general introduction to the topic to be investigated.
- Assign one specific aspect of the topic to each member of the group for in-depth exploration.
- Reorganize the groups so that all participants investigating one aspect of the topic are together. These become expert groups.
- Assign roles to each member of the expert groups:

recorder	runner	encourager
reader	observer	summarizer
checker		

- Provide the expert groups with any resources that may assist in their investigations.
- Allow the expert groups time to master their topics.
- Have members of the expert groups return to their home groups.
- Have each member of the home groups act as teacher to provide others with their expert information.

To provide flexibility the teacher may permit students to select the Engagement Activity they wish to complete for their book. In this case the teacher may need to group together students who are completing the same activity to increase their cooperative group opportunities, then monitor the groups to observe progress. The teacher may also permit students to work independently as they complete their activity. If this procedure is the choice of the teacher, she or he must make sure students possess know-how regarding the specific activity selected. Clearly, there are several means to achieve the desired end.

5. How can all students gain from a literature centered program?

Teachers must always be concerned about students of all ability levels when implementing a literature centered program. For instance, there are many alternatives that will provide less able readers with opportunities to respond to literature through Engagement Activities and to grow as readers:

- Provide titles at a variety of reading levels, including a number that are rated as below grade level.
- Plan teacher read alouds of books that are of the appropriate interest level but inappropriate readability levels.
- Provide taped books and a listening center.
- Recruit classroom volunteers who will assist less able readers.
- Make use of cross-age tutoring—older students with younger ones.

- Develop programs for Book Buddies, partners, and peer tutors.
- Provide Radio Reading activities (Greene, 1979).
- Provide Engagement Activities that allow for oral/artistic/dramatic responses (Cullinan, 1987, chapter 12).
- Build intrinsic motivation, focusing on existing student interests.
- Encourage risk taking and reduce the emphasis on being right.

6. How do you evaluate the effectiveness of a literature centered program?

Evaluation strategies are an essential part of any management system. They provide teachers, students, parents, and administrators with meaningful feedback related to student growth and current functioning level, program effectiveness, and teacher effectiveness. In addition, they identify strengths and weaknesses and build accountability into the program.

Good evaluation practices appropriate for literature centered programs do not differ from good evaluation practices in general. They are dependent upon a clear definition of goals that should have been identified before any instruction has taken place and an efficient data-gathering and record-keeping system. It is essential to decide how the program is to be evaluated before embarking on the activities. Only data that are absolutely necessary should be gathered, lest teachers risk data overload. The following are examples of evaluation strategies that are appropriate and meaningful:

- informal observation with anecdotal records
- individual conferences with anecdotal records
- collections of work samples
- checklists based on established goals and objectives of the program
- reading logs
- reading response journals
- reading folders
- response activities records
- pre- and postprogram tests and quizzes
- samples of student writing
- completion of evaluation tests on literature units

Data can be gathered by teachers, students, peers, parents, volunteers, teachers' aides, librarians, and administrators. Sample record-keeping systems can include reading logs, reading folders, and checklists. Ultimately, the teacher makes data-based judgments.

7. Once you have developed the program, how do you set up your classroom?

Teachers may have a number of questions related to the physical plan of the classroom, such as:

- "Will I need more room?…different furniture?…furniture moved about for different purposes and groupings?"
- "Where will all the books be kept?"
- "How do I provide space for group activities?"
- "What do I do about noise levels?"

Effective room arrangement should include:

- a reading area/center that is comfortable and fairly quiet, and that provides ready access to books and other reading materials;
- a writing area/center with individual desks, a work table, and a supply of writing, illustrating, and book-making materials;
- a large group area for discussion, drama, Reader's Theatre, etc.;
- a listening center with a record/tape player and headphones (if possible) and easy access to records, tapes, videos, related books, and other materials; and
- learning centers that are flexible and can be changed as needed.

Another key factor in classroom organization is the critical evaluation of existing furniture and equipment and its arrangement. A great deal of space can often be created by removing furniture and materials not essential to the planned curriculum. Some teachers find their desks unnecessary and gain considerable space by removing them.

8. How can you obtain more help for the classroom?

The development and use of human resources is an important management strategy. Teachers often feel alone and isolated in their classrooms, but this need not be the case. There are many people who can help make classroom programs manageable, such as:

- The students themselves. They are always there and their value as assistants should never be overlooked. They can act as Book Buddies, peer tutors, collaborators, partners, or merely "gofers."
- Fellow teachers. Colleagues can pair up to plan units, locate materials, raise funds, and provide moral support and encourgement.
- School librarians. Librarians have expertise and resources that can be invaluable to the teacher in developing literature centered programs.
- School administrators. Principals want to support worthwhile activities, and their interest and participation can be of great worth. They should be kept abreast of innovative classroom programs.

- Classroom volunteers. Members of the community such as retired educators, senior citizens, high school and college students, and housewives can be an invaluable resource, well worth the effort of recruiting and training.
- Teachers' aides. If instructional aides are available, they can provide consistent support in the implementation of a literature centered program.

References

Altwerger, B., Edelsky, C., & Flores, B. (1987). Whole language: What's new? *The Reading Teacher, 41,* 144-154.

Ammon, R. (1983). Evaluation in the holistic reading/language arts curriculum. In U.H. Hardt (Ed.), *Teaching reading with the other language arts*. Newark, DE: International Reading Association.

Anderson, R.C., & Pearson, P.D. (1984). A schema-theoretic view of basic processes in reading comprehension. In P.D. Pearson (Ed.), *Handbook of reading research*. New York: Longman.

Anderson, R.C., Hiebert, E.H., Scott, J.A., & Wilkinson, I.A.G. (1985). *Becoming a nation of readers: The report of the commission on reading*. Washington, DC: National Academy of Education, National Institute of Education, Center for the Study of Reading.

Barrett, F.L., Holdaway, D., Lynch, P., & Peetoom, A. (1983). *The three i's: A whole-language experience*. Richmond Hill, Ontario: Scholastic.

Brubacher, M., & Payne, R. (1985). The team approach to small group learning. *Highway One, 8,* 140-149.

California State Department of Education. (1987). *English-language arts framework*. Sacramento, CA.

Cullinan, B.E. (1987). Inviting readers to literature. In B.E. Cullinan (Ed.), *Children's literature in the reading program*. Newark, DE: International Reading Association.

Cullinan, B.E. (Ed.). (1987). *Children's literature in the reading program*. Newark, DE: International Reading Association.

Dishon, D., & O'Leary, P.W. (1984). *A guidebook for cooperative learning: A technique for creating more effective schools*. Portage, MI: Cooperation Unlimited.

Genishi, C., & Dyson, A. (1985). *Early language assessment*. Norwood, NJ: Ablex.

Greene, F. (1979). Radio reading. In C. Pennock (Ed.), *Reading comprehension at four linguistic levels*. Newark, DE: International Reading Association.

Henke, L. (1987). Beyond basal reading: A district's commitment to change. *The New Advocate, 1,* 42-51.

Intile, J.K., & Conrad, H. (1980). Planning the well managed classroom. In D. Lapp (Ed.), *Making reading possible through effective classroom management*. Newark, DE: International Reading Association.

Johnson, D.W., & Johnson, R.T. (1975). *Learning together and alone: Cooperation, competition, and individualization*. Englewood Cliffs, NJ: Prentice Hall.

Johnson, D.W., Johnson, R.T., Holubec, E.J., & Roy, P. (1986). *Circles of learning*. Englewood Cliffs, NJ: Prentice Hall.

Johnson, T.D. & Louis, D.R. (1987). *Literacy through literature*. Portsmouth, NH: Heinemann Educational Books.

Largent, M. (1986). *Response to literature: Moving towards an aesthetic transaction*. Unpublished manuscript, University of California, Berkeley.

Malloch, J., & Malloch, I. (1986). *Books alive: A literature-based integrated program*. Toronto, Ontario: Doubleday Canada.

Martin, B. (1987). The making of a reader: A personal narrative. In B.E. Cullinan (Ed.), *Children's literature in the reading program*. Newark, DE: International Reading Association.

Memory, D.M. (1980). Record keeping for effective reading instruction. In D. Lapp (Ed.), *Making reading possible through effective classroom management*. Newark, DE: International Reading Association.

Palincsar, A.S., & Brown, A.L. (1985). Reciprocal teaching: Activities to promote "reading with your mind." In T.L. Harris & E.J. Cooper (Eds.), *Reading, thinking, and concept development* (pp. 147-158). New York: College Board Publications.

Rhodes, L.K. (1983). Organizing the elementary classroom for effective language learning. In U.H. Hardt (Ed.), *Teaching reading with the other language arts*. Newark, DE: International Reading Association.

Rosenblatt, L. (1978). *The reader, the text, the poem: The transactional theory of the literary work*. Urbana, IL: National Council of Teachers of English.

Rosenblatt, L. (1985). The transactional theory of literary work: Implications for research. In C. Cooper (Ed.), *Researching response to literature and the teaching of literature*. Norwood, NJ: Ablex.

Sawyer, W. (1987). Literature and literacy: A review of research. *Language Arts, 64,* 33-39.

Tierney, R., & Pearson, P.D. (1985). Learning to learn from text: A framework for improving classroom practice. In H. Singer & R. Ruddell (Eds.), *Theoretical models and processes of reading*. Newark, DE: International Reading Association.

Whisler, N.G., & Williams, J.A. (1988, May). Promoting comprehension and cooperative learning from success in reading. (Available at 2020 7th Ave., Sacramento, CA 95818.) Microworkshop presented at the 33rd International Reading Association Convention, Toronto, Ontario.

Zakaluk, B.L., & Samuels, S.J. (Eds.). (1988). *Readability: Its past, present, and future*. Newark, DE: International Reading Association.